P

"Ingrid's inspiring journey of breaking old patterns and creating new ones beautifully illustrates the power of coaching and the potential that each of us possesses for transformation."
- Bruce D Schneider, Founder of iPEC Coaching and Author of *Energy Leadership*

"Childhood trauma undoubtedly profoundly impacts the lens through which one sees and operates in the world. Ingrid paints this picture while also showing that it is possible to move towards recovery and healing despite what occurred in the past. *Unmasked* is a beautiful story of hope and a journey towards healthy living despite a traumatic and painful past."
- Kylie Billingsley, PhD

"Ingrid Abild-Pedersen has so poignantly shared with us what was behind her mask, bravely stepping out of her comfort zone to show us how to do the same. May we all have the courage to step out from behind what binds us to develop into the people we were meant to be."
- Iris Kaddis, MD, Pediatrician, Northern California

"Raw, unfiltered, poignant look into the inner workings of trauma and all of the ways it tries to bleed the life out of a person. A triumphant journey out of the dark that will

inspire anyone impacted by trauma to believe that there is more to life than just what has happened to you."
- Rachel Grant, Sexual Abuse Recovery Coach & Author of *Beyond Surviving: The Final Stage in Recovery from Sexual Abuse*

"As a mental health provider for over 11 years, this work has reminded me of the body, mind, soul connection and the impossibility of healing when all are not treated. Healing is a progression as much as it is an event and that resonates true for most who have embarked on a similar journey. This book reminds us of what it means to begin on the journey, as we choose to do or not to do each day. An inspirational read for anyone who is sick and tired of being sick and tired."
- Tiffany Douglass, MA, Mental Health & Substance Abuse Subject Matter Expert

"A short and wholehearted read. Ingrid's vulnerability is profound from start to finish. She fosters connection with the reader and intertwines struggle with hope."
- Nicole Bahbout, Clinical Case Manager

"Ingrid Abild-Pedersen speaks from the most openhearted and vulnerable space, providing readers the courage to return to wholeness."
- Keith Miller

"*Unmasked* is a rare breed of story that connects us to the transformative possibility, which lies only within the arena of vulnerability. Indeed, Ingrid's journey is real-life evidence that there is so much more freedom waiting for you if you'd just let down your mask. It's a transformation so powerful you won't be able to put it down."
- Taylor Anna Garrett, Leadership Coach

"A raw and inspirational message of hope. Ingrid shares her heart with the readers and her expertise guides anyone who had to face trauma to find self-acceptance and love. A must-read."
- Dr. Fabienne Slama - FabYOUlicious - Core Emotional Awakening Coach

"It is rare to find a person willing to be as open, raw, and vulnerable as Ingrid is in her book. She shows what is possible for us as we navigate this messy life, learning to let go of the past, fully feeling and embracing pain, and triumphantly stepping into our power."
- Kristin Paga, RN, BSN

"A captivating book on the quest for self, the desperate search for happiness and the ability to rebuild oneself, thanks to the support of loved ones, resilience, and hope, after having suffered from an old trauma. Ingrid Abild-Pedersen's book will help and inspire those of us who feel stuck and look for a change in their lives."
- Sixtine Gontier, Life-College and Career Coach

"As a nurse and a patient, it's easy to feel that the health system may fail some. Ingrid's message is one that is deeply and tremendously necessary! She provides a clear voice and reminder on the importance of treating the whole patient, including acknowledging past emotional, physical, and mental scars."

- Natalie Siemers, BSN, RN

"This book shares such an authentic and vulnerable journey. We all have some degree of trauma in our lives. Ingrid walks us through how with persistence, even our deepest trauma can be healed."

- Mary Kay Garrett, Parenting Coach at Raising Remarkable Kids

"*Unmasked* is a gripping, vulnerable, and eye-opening view of what drives us to do what we do. Ingrid is courageous and raw, showing the journey in detail that is humanizing. If you want to see and accept yourself more clearly to live free, let go of the mask."

- Kevin Eyres, Conscious Leadership Coach, Teacher, and Speaker

"This intriguing, honest, transparent book takes the readers on a journey from heartache to triumph. The author leaves no detail out to get across her viewpoint of how she overcame the emotional ups and downs in her own life, only to come out the other side a more resilient and connected human being. A valuable characteristic for anyone who has had similar experiences in their own lives."

- Melissa Dandeneau, life coach, registered nurse

"Ingrid is an incredible mentor who exemplifies what it is to be a strong, caring leader guiding the way for others towards personal peace and fulfillment. Her illuminating memoir is delightfully raw and refreshing as she shares her intimate experience of the struggle with wanting love, yet locking herself away in addiction. Ingrid's writing is compelling and engaging. I know this is only the first of many more amazing storytellings to come!"

- Whitney Walker, LMFT and Founder of Women Waken

"I was hooked when reading *Unmasked*. It was hard to put the book down! It gave me another perspective of my own previous trauma that I have never had before! I am truly grateful for this read and highly recommend it!"

- Desiree LeVeira-Ferguson, Pet Bereavement Specialist & Social Work Student

UN MASKED

A Triumphant Memoir of Recovery from Childhood Trauma, Eating Disorder, and PTSD

INGRID CHRISTINE ABILD-PEDERSEN

Copyright © 2022 Ingrid Christine Abild-Pedersen

All rights reserved. No part of this book may be used or reproduced in any manner without written permission from the author and publisher, except by reviewers, bloggers or other individuals who may quote brief passages, as long as they are clearly credited to the author.

Neither the publisher nor the author is engaged in rendering professional advice or services to the individual reader. The ideas and suggestions contained in this book are not intended as a substitute for professional help. Neither the author nor the publisher shall be liable or responsible for any loss or damage allegedly arising from any information or suggestion in this book.

The events in this book are true to the best of the author's memory. Some names and identifying details have been changed to protect the privacy of parties involved. Additionally, any views expressed in this book are solely the author's and not intended to represent any company, corporation, or brand other than her own.

Capucia LLC
211 Pauline Drive #513
York, PA 17402
www.capuciapublishing.com
Send questions to: support@capuciapublishing.com

Paperback ISBN: 978-1-954920-38-5
eBook ISBN: 978-1-954920-39-2
Library of Congress Control Number: 2022913967

Cover Design: Ranilo Cabo
Layout: Ranilo Cabo
Editor and Proofreader: Simon Whaley
Book Midwife: Karen Everitt
Author Photo: Teresa Nora Trobbe www.FotosbyT.com

Printed in the United States of America

Capucia LLC is proud to be a part of the Tree Neutral® program. Tree Neutral offsets the number of trees consumed in the production and printing of this book by taking proactive steps such as planting trees in direct proportion to the number of trees used to print books. To learn more about Tree Neutral, please visit treeneutral.com.

Disclaimer
This book deals with childhood trauma, self-harm, drug abuse, rape, and mental health issues. While the author has worked to ensure the subject matter is dealt with in a respectful and compassionate manner, the content may be troubling for some readers. Discretion is advised.

To my family
Cilia, Jonas, and Frank

CONTENTS

Forewords   1

Introduction   5

Chapter 1   The Mask   9

Chapter 2   The Eating Disorder   15

Chapter 3   Therapists   25

Chapter 4   The Forgotten Trauma   33

Chapter 5   The Breakdown   39

Chapter 6   The Crossroad/The Change   47

Chapter 7   Marriage and Family Life   51

Chapter 8   My Thoughts   59

Chapter 9   Aftermath   65

Acknowledgments   69

About the Author   73

FOREWORDS

We are captivated by stories in which individuals face incredible trials in their quest to overcome villains and monsters. In mythological tales, individuals embark on a quest called the "hero's journey" as described by the author Joseph Campbell. This "journey" is the currency of legendary tales which appear within every culture, every generation, and every historical time. Our hero-to-be in these accountings is an individual with whom we can often identify because their suffering in some ways mirrors our own, yet we can only hope to persevere similarly like they do as they rise to engage their adversaries.

Each of us has the capacity to be on a "hero's journey" of self-discovery. Most who choose this path do not become famous or legendary, but that is not important as this is not the goal of the seeker. The seeker desires liberation—freedom from one's nemesis, whether it be the seven-headed dragon of folklore, or for many, the hidden demons which lurk in the recesses of our minds, hidden even from our own awareness. Such demons may be our punishing thoughts, memories, and beliefs that tell us we are defective, unworthy, or unlovable.

Whatever the adversary, nonetheless, it must be metaphorically slayed or tamed.

I have had the pleasure and honor of knowing Ingrid Abild-Pedersen in my capacity as a medical school professor involved in courses on behavioral medicine, psychiatry, and the human side of medicine.

Ingrid's personal story, which she shares so generously with eager medical students, begins as a young woman who recognized the depths of her own despair and through her curiosity, raw honesty, and courage was able to uncover and confront her past, thereby transforming destructive beliefs and behaviors from running her life… and from ruining her life.

I watch as students are fully engaged and deeply appreciative whilst Mrs. Abild-Pedersen speaks eloquently of her life challenges and of how she overcame her own trials of adversity.

Her story inspires and illuminates the quest for wholeness and happiness that we all desire.

My sincere hope is that she can reach and touch many others through the telling of her powerful story.

Martin Rubin, MD
American Board of Psychiatry and Neurology

FOREWORDS

In the fall of 2017, I accepted a position as psychiatry clerkship director for a brand-new medical school, California Northstate University College of Medicine. Tasked with having to provide a taste of the thrills and chills of psychiatry to half a dozen almost-doctors at a time, I set up their month-long mental health curriculum, eager to locate dynamic speakers. I learned about Ingrid Abild-Pedersen from another faculty member.

"She's a Life Coach in the San Francisco Bay Area with a passion for teaching," he told me. "What's more, she has a great story to tell."

I'm always a sucker for a good story. After my first extended phone call with Ingrid, I was convinced that she would, indeed, become a treasured resource. From the start, Ingrid impressed me with her passion and commitment to the students. She did not balk when I informed her she would have to make the 200-mile round trip drive to Elk Grove each month (without reimbursement) to share her story with only two to six medical students at a time.

Ingrid was an enthusiastic "guinea pig" for the students. She painstakingly answered all their questions as they developed their skills in taking an appropriate mental health history. The icing on the cake occurred after all their questions dried up, and she then related the complete, no-holds-barred, full story of her life. The students sat riveted on their seats as they realized their questions had only brushed the surface of her complex history. It was a wonderful opportunity for them to learn, firsthand, the nuances and complexities one navigates in order to perform a thorough mental health history. Her talk was always ranked very highly by the students. They shared with me that they appreciated her honesty and courage in sharing such intensely personal details for their own education.

Ingrid describes in this memoir how she embarked on a road that was poised to terminate at an ill-fated destination. Instead, the reader is given a gripping portrayal of how she broke out of the trauma cycle to chart a new course, while at the same time she developed immense courage and resilience along the way. The meat of this story will likely remain in your consciousness long after you put this book down. I endorse this work without reservation and hope it will act as a beacon of light for others who have experienced similar challenges in their own lives.

    Lally Pia, MD
    Child and Adolescent Psychiatry
    River Oak Center for Children

INTRODUCTION

Journal Entry, 1992
I look happy on the outside. But inside I feel sad, lonely, lost, and overwhelmed. I am not good enough.

Many people live their life sometimes feeling overwhelmed, angry, depressed, anxious, worried, or sad. These are all normal feelings, and we all have them. But they can, for some adults, also be triggered by childhood trauma and become so intense that these feelings take over their life.

Many people have experienced some kind of childhood trauma, and it can really mess up their thoughts and belief system enough to make them seek professional help.

Furthermore, many people frequently see their doctor with physical symptoms like fatigue, concentration problems, chronic pain, racing heartbeat, and many other stress-related symptoms. I believe that some physical symptoms are also related to childhood trauma, and by overlooking that, the patient can be stuck in a medical system for years, if not for life.

In general, we need to talk more openly about the effect that childhood trauma has on a person's life as an adult.

By understanding more about the connection between childhood trauma, mental health, and physical symptoms, we can help more people break the traumatic and abusive cycle so they can heal and live a life as a person instead of a patient. For example, a parent's childhood trauma can be triggered when their own child reaches the age they were when the trauma occurred. Or the fact that many relationships could be saved if a person looked at their own history instead of focusing on trying to change their partner.

Childhood trauma can be many things, and it looks different for every person. But how does it affect us when we grow up? And how do we get out of it?

In my job as a life and relationship coach, I have, over the years, seen many beautiful and smart people who, as adults, for different reasons, are stuck in past pain and hurt. This holds them back from believing in themselves and living their life. They often react to people or situations in very intense ways and cope by numbing themselves or by self-sabotaging.

Many of my clients have seen a therapist before they come to me. Typically, they have been happy working with their therapist, but they still feel stuck in the victim mode and are ready to try something new. Others have been treated by doctors for their physical symptoms, but they don't seem to get better. Many times, the doctors only focus on the physical symptoms instead of looking at the overall picture of a patient's life.

Before becoming a life and relationship coach, I spent many years in therapy myself. I received treatment for

INTRODUCTION

an eating disorder and post-traumatic stress (PTSD). But even though I worked on myself for many years, there was still a missing link I had overlooked. My body had tried to communicate with me for several years, but I had not paid attention. What I did not know at the time was that childhood trauma was manifesting itself in my body as physical symptoms. I saw several doctors, but nobody connected the dots.

After several years of trying to find the cause of my physical symptoms, the doctors finally diagnosed me with a rare kind of Dystonia (Focal Dystonia, explained more in Chapter 4) and gave me medication to help me manage the symptoms. But nobody could explain why I had it or tell me how to cure it. Only when I changed myself did my physical symptoms disappear. The body and mind are connected.

I realized I had been trapped in old trauma for most of my life. Even though I had spent years in therapy and worked on myself, I still had a hard time living my life and feeling happy. I constantly blamed things or people from the past. Emotionally, I reacted as if I was still living it. I believed I was a victim. I even wrote a whole book about the trauma I had been through. On my way to publishing the book, I realized that this was not the book I needed to publish. Had I done so, it would have just kept me stuck in a blame cycle, and that was not what I wanted. Instead, I wanted to inspire others to let go of their past pain and hurt. I had felt first-hand how important that had been in my life. So, I started writing a new book—the book that you are reading right now.

This is not a book about my trauma or about who did what. Instead, this is a book to show how I reacted to childhood trauma. It's about how I was stuck in pain and suffering, the ugly side of my eating disorder and PTSD. It describes the transformation from victimhood to victory. Simply said, it's the journey I went through to get where I am today, where I finally feel free and happy.

If you have experienced trauma in your life, remember this—it was not your fault! I feel for you, and I know that many days are really hard. Nevertheless, as adults, it is important to heal from it so the past doesn't ruin our life now. This is especially important if you are a parent. It is our responsibility to break patterns and change things. We must stop cycles of abuse and trauma.

We can be stuck in suffering, negativity, trauma, and sickness. But we only have one life, so every moment counts. Life happens to us all. Trauma is not a competition of who has the hardest life. Life can be tough, but it can also be extremely beautiful. It's all about what we focus on and how we respond to life. We don't have to live in pain and suffering. My goal with this book is to give you the hope and courage to let go of your past pain so that you can finally live the life that you deserve.

Going through childhood trauma makes us strong, and I wish for you to find your own strength and resilience as you read this book.

We all have a choice. Change is hard work, but I know you can do it. I believe in you!

CHAPTER 1

The Mask

Journal Entry, 2020
I am sick of hiding and pretending. I have not done anything else all my life. It is a prison, an emotional prison, and I believe I have served my time. It is now my time to leave the prison. It is my time to start living. I am letting go of the mask.

Nearly all my life, I have been living behind a mask. A mask that covered up the childhood trauma I experienced. A mask that hid the real me. All my life, I have been the good girl. I have done all I can to live up to others' expectations, to fit in the box, and to please everybody around me. I desperately needed them to like me, or just see me or hear me.

The thing is, though, I hated myself. The trauma I experienced made me think I was not beautiful enough, not smart enough, not sexy enough, etc. I was just not good enough! I did all I could to avoid those feelings and thoughts. I coped by numbing them in any way I could, or I self-sabotaged by harming myself to feel the extreme. I stayed busy and lived my life on autopilot. That way, I didn't have to deal with my issues and feelings that I did not want anybody else, or even myself, to know about. From the outside, everything looked great. I appeared happy, successful, and if you saw me, you would think that my life was perfect. What you did not see was the daily pain, nor the physical and emotional suffering, that was making my life hellish to live. I needed a mask to cover up the real me. But the mask was crumbling, and I was slowly drowning.

I have always had a difficult time figuring out who I am. Growing up, I spent a lot of my time performing on stage, either acting, singing, or dancing ballet. On the stage, I felt safe. There was a script. I knew what role to play. It was very different from my real life. When I was on stage, I could pretend to be somebody else, and I could allow myself to show the character's emotions and feelings. I loved it! Of course, there were times when I was nervous about performing and afraid of forgetting my lines. But as soon as I stepped onto the stage and felt the lights and saw the audience, I relaxed. On stage, I was pretending to be somebody else, yet I was also more honest on stage than in my real life. Here, I could love, hate, be curious, and be alive—all the things I struggled with in my real life. Offstage, I felt like hiding. I was confused, scared, and insecure, but I did not show it or tell anybody.

The mask worked well in my younger days, but when I grew older, my emotions grew in size and strength. It became more difficult for me to push away those unwanted feelings, like loneliness, anger, or sadness. In the years right after high school, I traveled and jobbed around Denmark, Germany, and England. The feeling of loneliness was often especially overwhelming, so to get through the day, I would often numb myself with alcohol, drugs, sex, or simply being busy. My romantic relationships seldomly lasted long. I had lots of one-night stands, or I had sex partners. Sex was like an addiction to me. It made me feel good and wanted.

Journal Entry, 1994
Last night I went to a pub, and I had too much to drink. I felt lonely and joined a young man back at his home, and we started making out. At some point, I did not feel like being there anymore, and I told him we should stop. I wanted to go home. But he did not stop. I told him again, louder. Still, he did not stop. Now I started panicking. He held me down and said he wanted to be with me. I begged him to stop, and I tried kicking him off me. But he was stronger and just laughed. He tried to get into me. I did all I could to stop him, but he became more desperate. On the table beside the bed, there was a bottle of shower gel. He opened it and sprayed it in my vagina to make it easier for him to enter me. He forced himself in. The soap inside me burned and stung, but I couldn't do anything else other than wait for him to finish.

Afterward, I went home and sat for a long time in the bathtub, crying. I was confused about what had happened.

For many years, I did not tell anybody about this incident. Instead, I just did what I always did. I blamed myself.

I had no idea what I wanted with my life. I just lived from one moment to the next without a plan. The only constant was this feeling of loneliness I had inside me. I did not want to feel it, so I continued living a life out of control. I drank alcohol, sniffed poppers, smoked marijuana, went to ecstasy parties, and had sex with strangers to get away from the feeling of loneliness that continued to overwhelm me. I knew it was a risky lifestyle, but I did not care. I needed to escape.

Journal Entry, 1994
It is 5 am. I wake up and look around. I am in a dark basement somewhere in England. Beside me in bed is a young man. It is dark. I cannot see a lot. I feel tired and sore. I am naked. I remember sniffing poppers with him and having the most fantastic sex last night. We ended the night smoking a joint together. I don't really know him. We met at a party. I felt attracted to him, and I wanted him. I do not remember where he lives, where this basement is. I only remember that it felt amazing being with him. It felt electric when he touched me, and I wanted more of it.

"Good morning," says a deep voice.

He turns towards me. I cannot see him. It is still too dark.

I feel his moist lips kiss me on the right side of my head, his warm wet tongue moves around my ear. I can feel his breath. It gets heavier. It turns me on. My body longs for his beautiful, big hands to touch me again, so I move closer to him. I am longing for him to lick me. I feel his hands on my breasts. My nipples are hard and pointy. They feel sore from last night, but it doesn't matter. I want more. I want to fuck him. I want him to fuck me. His fingers are now playing with my wet vagina. Inside. Outside. I am hungry for more. He takes one of my hands up to the corner of the bed. I hear a click, and my arm is locked in a handcuff. He takes the other hand to the other side and the same thing happens. I cannot move my arms anymore.

It is still dark in the room. I can just see the sun rising behind the curtain by the window.

I feel his breath and his tongue playing around between my legs. He knows exactly what he is doing, and I enjoy every moment. My breathing gets stronger and heavier. I love it. I am so close to coming, and then he pulls away from me.

"Don't stop," I beg. I feel his touch all over my body, circling my breasts, and my stomach, down my legs. Then he comes back to my vagina, and I purr like a cat. His tongue is amazing. Then he stops again. I need him.

"I want you," he whispers gently in my ear.

Oh yes, please. My body is nearly electric.

He goes on top of me, and I can feel how turned on he is. His cock is so stiff and hard, it feels so strong and good. He fucks me. He fucks me hard. My hands are still in handcuffs. I don't want it to stop; I want more. And then I come—I scream so loud, and it feels so freeing. He lets me have a little break and then he starts fucking me again. I can feel his sweaty body. He is just gorgeous! And he fucks like a dream. He moves quicker, harder, his breath is strong and heavy, he calls me the most disgustingly sexy things. He is so ready now, and I am so ready, and this time we both come at the same time. We both scream out the satisfaction. We don't care who can hear us. We both love to fuck and to come, and we are both in heaven right now. It is beautiful and raw at the same time.

He frees me from the handcuffs, then jumps out of bed and opens the curtain. The light comes in through the window and the sun shines on his well-built naked body. He takes out a joint from his bag and jumps back into bed, where he lights it, and we share it. I look around the room; it is very messy here. It looks like a whole apartment in one room. A little kitchen, a living room area, a bedroom, and, in one corner, a shower.

"Do you want to join me for some breakfast in town?" he asks. "I need to bring something to a friend."

I smile. "Sure." I take another puff of the joint.

It was easy for me to mix up love and sex. I absorbed any kind of attention that I could get, and I thought that people would love me if I gave them sex. So, I was desperately looking for acceptance and love everywhere, and I knew how to play the game. Having one-night stands felt good in the moment. The loneliness always came back, though. But this way, I could be with somebody without revealing who I really was. Without looking at the true me. This way, I continued wearing the mask.

CHAPTER 2

The Eating Disorder

Even as a child, my feelings often overwhelmed me. I tried to be the perfect daughter. My parents had gotten a divorce when I was about three years old. In the family, I took on the role of Little Ms. Sunshine, trying to light up everybody's mood when things were hard. I took this role very seriously, so much so that I ended up losing myself. It meant more to me to help the people around me than it did to take care of myself. I did not want to let anybody down. I never really learned how to deal with the difficult emotions that were overwhelming me, so I just continued to push them away.

But when I was eleven years old, it all became too much for me. I needed to find an outlet for my emotions. Inside, I felt like such a failure, but I did not want to let anybody down. It seemed like it all had to look nice from the outside, which is why I wore a mask. It helped me hide my true feelings. One of the ways I coped with those feelings at that time was to binge eat and then throw up afterward. It was disgusting and painful, but the release I got from it was just what I needed. In the beginning, I only did it occasionally, but as time passed, this became my go-to thing. It was a way to get rid of those hard feelings—for a little while. It was never about wanting to lose weight or look good. For me, it was purely a way of giving my overwhelming emotions an outlet. This felt like something I could control.

I hid this side of me for many years. I felt it worked. In a way, I was scared to grow up. Somehow, inside me, I never really felt loved. I needed unconditional love. I needed to know that I was good enough, not just when I performed well. But I felt that nobody loved me, even though I tried so hard to be there for everybody else. The emotional pain just grew bigger and bigger. It felt like it was holding me hostage.

When I moved out after high school, I found other ways to deal with my emotions, along with the throwing up. I went from one addiction to another: sex, drugs, and alcohol. When I was with a man, or I was high, or drunk, I felt happy and loved. I lived for these moments.

After several years of partying and escaping myself and real life, I moved to Copenhagen to study. Not because I wanted to. I still did not know what I wanted to do with my life. I did it because I felt it was expected of me. It was something you did at my age, and all my friends from high school were already studying.

In Copenhagen, I lived in a dormitory, which is where I met Frank, a young guy who also lived there. We became good friends, and at some point, we started dating. He liked me a lot, which was very scary for me. It wasn't just about sex, though. He liked me as a person. I was terrified of what he would think about me if he knew the real me. Since the age of eleven, I had hidden the throwing up, but now, and especially because I was hanging out with Frank so much, it became more difficult to hide that side of me.

Journal Entry, 1997
I go to the bathroom and close the door. I stick a finger down my throat. I need to throw up. I hurt so much inside I need to get the pain out. I feel trapped in my feelings. They are so painful. I hate myself. I hate throwing up, but it brings me relief from feeling the pain. The taste of the vomit is disgusting, and my throat burns like it is on fire. I fall on the bathroom floor and cry like a little baby.

Frank knocks on the door, but I continue to cry. The door is not locked, and he comes in. He sits with me and comforts me, putting my head on his lap. He has seen me this way a few times before. I know it hurts him to see me like this, but he doesn't know what to do to help me. Frank loves me, but this side of me scares him.

The throwing up had gotten worse. At this point, it was difficult just drinking a glass of water without it coming up by itself. I lived with these crazy rituals. I tried all I could to have some kind of control. On my way home from school, I always stopped at a certain shop and bought a special kind of tortellini. If they were out of stock, I panicked. I needed them. The first thing I did when I came home was make a double portion of them. Often, I was in a kind of manic state. Nothing could come in my way. I ate them with a ton of butter. If I did not have any tortellini, I ate dough that I made from butter, sugar, and flour. I would eat a whole bowl of it, raw, and drink a lot of water or have ice cream with it. After binging, I would go to the restroom to throw up. And then I would typically lay down on my bed for a while. I frequently experienced stomach pains, headaches, and dizziness. Frank did not understand what was happening to me, and I could tell he was becoming concerned. We argued a lot during this time, mostly because of my emotional ups and downs. I was not feeling well at all.

Journal Entry, 1997
"What are you looking at?" I ask. "I know you are hiding something from me. Is there another woman in your life?"

My paranoid questions drive Frank crazy. He tries to understand that it has nothing to do with him, but he gets so hurt when I accuse him of all these different things.

"What is it?" I scream louder. My eyes bulge, practically sticking out of my head like a sharp weapon as I stare at him.

Frank does not know how to react. "There is nobody else," he says, trying to calm me down.

I feel my blood flowing around my body, faster and faster. It is like watching a horse race. I start sweating. The pain inside me is growing. The kettle is boiling. I look at him. My eyes are like burning statues right now.

"You don't love me anymore!" I yell as loud as I can. The pain comes all the way from the deepest pit of my stomach. I reach out to a book and throw it on the floor.

Frank looks at me. He doesn't know what to do. "What the hell is going on with you?"

I feel like I am going crazy. My hands try to hug him. "Help me," I whisper. "I am so angry."

Frank is conflicted. On the one hand, he is so disturbed about my accusing him of all these different things and getting angry with him. Yet, on the other hand, he knows that this has absolutely nothing to do with him, and he wants to help me. But it is hard to help me when he feels so badly treated by me. He just sits there, trying to figure out what to do.

"There, you see? You don't love me. You are not helping me!" I scream.

One evening, I took a knife into the bathroom because my feelings were so overwhelming. I didn't want to hurt myself. I was just scared, and I had never felt as low as this. Frank waited patiently on the other side of the bathroom door, talking to me in a calm voice, asking me to please come out. I sat on the floor, crying hysterically, and looked at the knife. I couldn't take it anymore. I listened to his voice and finally opened the door. He hugged me for several minutes. When I had calmed down, he looked at me and said, "You are a really nice girl, but if we are going to be together, then you should see a doctor."

The next day, I sat in the doctor's office. The doctor called me in and asked how I was doing.

"I am fine," I replied, as I walked into the exam room with him. When I sat down on the chair, I became quiet and looked down at the floor. After a few moments, I looked him in the eyes and whispered, "Actually, I am not feeling too well." I confessed that I had daily stomach pain, anxiety, and dizziness. I also mentioned the situation with the knife the day before, and that Frank had asked me to go to the doctor. After a physical exam and some ordinary questions, he asked if I was also throwing up. I was surprised to hear his question. How did he know? I felt ashamed but admitted to it.

The doctor shared with me some information about eating disorders called bulimia and anorexia. For me, throwing up had just been my way of taking control and dealing with difficult emotions. But over the years, it had become a habit. He told me about an eating disorder treatment that he wanted me to go to.

"But there is a waiting list," he said. "In the meantime, I want you to come here every week and talk to me until we can get you into treatment. And I need you to eat. If you weigh less than fifty kilograms, they will hospitalize you instead," he continued.

Every week I booked a time to see my doctor. In the beginning, I did not understand why I should go and talk to him every week. What would we talk about? But, very quickly, I understood the benefit of it. He asked me different questions about my life and then he would listen. Sometimes I cried, but that was okay. He would still listen. It felt good to talk to him. I was so lucky to have a doctor who just totally understood what I needed, was willing to see me as the person I was, and take the time to talk to me until he could get me into treatment. He clearly cared about me.

After a few months, I was at the top of the waiting list and it was time for me to go on the scales in his office. I was very nervous. I had tried eating, but everything would come up again right away. What started with me taking the only control I could when I was eleven years old was now a habit that was controlling me. I slowly stepped onto the scales and closed my eyes. I had stones in my pocket. I just needed to weigh fifty kilograms.

The treatment my doctor had been talking about was an outpatient treatment program at a hospital in Copenhagen. It was a combination of group therapy and individual therapy. I was in a group with five to six other young adult females who also had an eating disorder. I was amazed and scared at the same time. All this time I had been alone with all my difficult feelings, and now I realized there were other people with the same kind of disturbing thoughts. One after the other told stories about their lives and shared how they did not like themselves and how they had been dealing with it so far. *I was not alone.*

Being in the group was such a new world for me. I liked the other group members, and we built up a very close bond. We became each other's biggest support and cheered each other on. We could tell the group everything that was on our minds. In the beginning, that was very hard for me, because I had lived with my mask for so many years. I thought that things always had to look nice and happy from the outside. But here in the group, I could share how I really felt. I did not have to smile and pretend. I did not have to lie. All of us had experienced some kind of abuse or trauma. Listening to the other group members share their stories gave me the courage to open up about my own experiences. Nothing was taboo here. We shared everything, and we cried and laughed together. I had found a place for me to fit in.

After group therapy sessions, we had lunch. Many of us struggled with this eating together, which was why they had us practice it. For me, the hardest part was to stop throwing up afterward. It had been my way of dealing with my feelings for so long and now, when I was not allowed to throw up, I did not know what to do. Many difficult emotions began to surface.

Journal Entry, 1998
"What are you looking at?" I ask Frank, as he sits at his computer.

"Nothing," he says. Quickly, he closes it down. He can see that I am in one of those moments where it does not matter what he says. I will find something to get angry with him about.

I feel very insecure, very jealous, and very lonely. All these feelings make it difficult for me to trust him, to trust anybody. I am not allowed to throw up, but I am just so angry. Sometimes, I let it out on Frank. He understands it is because of things I am dealing with in therapy, but it is very hard on the relationship right now. I am suspicious about anything, and I see ghosts everywhere. My insecurity and fear of losing him show up like a tornado and I accuse him of the worst things ever. When we walk together on the street, he feels very uncomfortable, because I will be upset and angry if he just looks at another girl walking by. I am so paranoid at the moment.

Frank feels trapped by my anger outbursts. They can destroy a whole evening, and yet he has done nothing wrong.

It is all in my head. I know I am not treating him well at the moment. I know I am doing a lot of things wrong, and my biggest fear is that he will leave me. I am such a big mess and failure.

The more I talked about stuff in therapy, the angrier I became. I started yelling at Frank. I smashed plates, and sometimes I was totally out of control. I had never been so angry before. Frank came with me to some therapy sessions, where they explained to him that I was dealing with a lot of old stuff. He was the most patient and understanding boyfriend that anybody could have wished for. He gave me something I had never had—he believed in me, unconditionally. He saw me and accepted me for who I was.

CHAPTER 3

Therapists

During the eating disorder treatment, I learned a lot about myself and was given some tools to help me deal with the difficult feelings. Even though I felt stronger when the treatment ended, I still experienced emotional challenges and, at some point, I felt I needed to talk to somebody again. I found a therapist. Her office was dark and very cluttered, and her dog was always snoring during our sessions. She wanted me to take some antidepressants. I agreed, but I did not feel comfortable taking them.

Journal Entry, 1999
I ring the doorbell, and Karen opens the door.

Karen has been my therapist for a while now. Today, Frank is joining me for the session. Karen wants to meet him. Frank does not really want to go, but he will do anything to help me get better.

"Hi, Karen. This is Frank." I am excited that he is here with me.

They shake hands, and we all walk into her office. The office is packed with big heavy furniture, plants, and many old pictures. Karen sits down at a big desk full of papers. Frank and I take the seats on the other side. Just by our feet, in front of the big heavy desk, we see Karen's little dog sleeping in a dog bed.

"How are you doing today?" Karen asks me.

I explain about a conversation I have had with someone that has made me feel very uncomfortable and very guilty.

Karen listens to me and hands me a tissue when I cry. I sob, and Frank puts his arm around me to comfort me. The dog wakes up and looks around. He gets up and slowly walks out of the room.

"How is the medication working?" Karen asks.

I have been taking the antidepressants for a while now, but I do not feel a big difference. I explain to her my concerns about the side effects and tell her that I would like to stop taking them. They don't seem to help my depression anyway, I explain.

"I think you should continue taking them," she says, and then turns to Frank.

"So, Frank. Tell me a little about you," she says, leaning back in her chair with her arms crossed.

Frank tells her about himself and answers politely her questions about his family background.

Frank's family has welcomed me in such a loving way, even though I have been having a hard time. I have enjoyed getting to know them. Sometimes it has been overwhelming for me to visit them because I cannot believe they can be so nice and actually like me for who I am. Sometimes I become jealous when we visit them and, as a result of the hard, intense emotions, I start a fight with Frank. I explain to Karen how it can be difficult for me that they are so nice to me. And I cry again. I cry a lot.

She looks up at both of us and then she blames Frank for some of my pain. I don't really understand what she means. How can he be the cause of my pain right now?

Frank looks at Karen and then at me. He is very confused.

During the rest of the session, Karen tells me about how I can get the comfort that I need so much from nature. Every time I feel sad, I should go outside and find a tree and hug it. That, together with the medication, would make it all better.

Frank and I leave the session very frustrated. We decide to go to a café. Frank orders the coffee, and we sit down on a nice couch. He looks at me. My eyes are all red and swollen from the crying. It doesn't matter to him. He just loves me and wants to do everything he can to help me. We take a sip of our coffee.

I feel overwhelmingly tired and my head hurts. We look at each other. Frank is nervous. I try to remember what Karen had said, and I attempt to understand it. How can Frank cause me all that pain?

Suddenly, I laugh out loud. Very loud. Hysterically loud. People at the other tables look at me, and Frank looks at me. Now we both laugh, with tears rolling down our cheeks.

After a few minutes of laughing, I look at Frank seriously. "I should go and hug a tree? You must be kidding me. There is no way I will hug a tree!" I cry out loud and laugh again.

Frank looks at me and smiles. He knows that this is a hard time for us, but deep inside all this mess, there is this woman that he loves with all his heart, and he will do all he can to help me out. "We will be ok," he says and kisses me gently.

"And you know what, Frank? I will stop taking the antidepressants and I will find a new therapist. This is just not working. There must be another way."

We finish our coffee and walk out of the café, holding hands. I know that Frank is good for me. We love each other the best we can now, both of us knowing that we have a long and bumpy road ahead of us. But we are both very determined to go that way together.

"There is a tree," says Frank. "Do you want to hug it?"

I laugh. Frank loves to hear me laugh like that. We walk home hand in hand.

I stopped taking the medication and stopped seeing Karen. Instead, I went to my own doctor, who I trusted, and asked him if he knew a therapist that would be good for me. And yes, he did.

Journal Entry, 1999
I stand in front of a big building, in one of the smaller streets in the heart of Copenhagen. I ring the doorbell and the door opens. When I walk in, I see a beautiful staircase, and I walk up the stairs until I reach the third floor. There it is. I open the door and walk in. To the right, there is a waiting area with some chairs and small tables with magazines. I take a seat in the chair by the window and look around. There are pictures on the walls, some of them are of girls in ballet costumes, some of beautiful nature. All the colors are calming, and it feels relaxing and safe to be here. I take a magazine and start looking through it. I cannot concentrate, so I put it away again. My hands are cold and sweaty at the same time. I am nervous.

I hear a door open and some footsteps come closer. My heart beats faster. I can nearly hear it.

"Are you Ingrid?" A man stands at the door and looks at me.
"Yes," I stutter.

THERAPISTS

"Wonderful. I am Christian. Welcome, I will be with you in a minute, ok?"

I nod, and he walks away. I look up at the picture with the ballet girl, and I think back to the time when I used to dance. What has happened? I feel tears fighting their way into my eyes. "Don't cry now," I think, but I cannot help it. The tears are rolling down my face. I try to wipe them away with my hand, but they just keep coming. Like a faucet that is broken, and the water just runs out.

I look up, and Christian is now standing beside me. He gives me a paper towel. "Here," he says. "It is totally fine. You can cry here. Let's go into my office, shall we?"

I walk with him up the hall and into a nice, light room. At the window, there is a big comfy chair.

"You can sit there," he says and points to it.

I sit down and look around. It is a pleasant room, with plants, books, a sofa, some chairs, a desk, some nice lights.

"I am Christian," he said, smiling at me. "I know it has been a rough time for you, and I am so happy you are here. I will help you to feel better."

Now I cannot hold it back any longer. I sob with all my heart. I feel so relieved to be here, even though I don't know Christian or anything about how he works. But I can just feel that he is going to help me. Finally.

Christian gives me time and space to cry. He somehow understands my pain. I have tried other therapists, but Christian is different, and I feel very comfortable with him.

My eating disorder diagnosis gave me an identity, and at the same time, the feeling that somebody was taking care of me. The support group had been like a safety net. It gave me the validation and attention that I had been seeking. They saw me and heard me. But, in a way, having the diagnosis also made me feel trapped in my own sickness. I often used it as an excuse for not taking responsibility. For not living my life.

Christian's way of helping me see my life and the things I was dealing with was very different from what I had been used to. He was tough and caring at the same time. Every time I blamed somebody for things like, "then they made me feel so angry that ..." he would reframe it into "You let them make you feel angry," and I would get so annoyed with him. I was used to therapists just sitting and nodding, telling me they understood, but Christian really pushed me to understand that I had power over my own feelings and thoughts.

He told me that I could stay like this forever and feel sorry for myself, or I could start doing something about it. Many times, I would use my eating disorder as an excuse for not changing, but he challenged me every time. Wow! His approach was so provocative and different. I needed to hear what he said (many times) to wake up. And he was right. I could continue to blame myself and everybody else forever, but that did not help me get rid of the pain inside. I needed to let go and move forward.

One of Christian's specialties was hypnosis, and at some point, I asked if he could help me try to remember more things since there was so much that I did not remember. He said no. He did not want to because he was scared of what might come up, and he did not think I was strong enough emotionally.

"You don't remember for a reason, and I don't think you are ready," he said. (And he was so right).

Instead, he wanted to give me some hypnosis to build up my self-esteem, so we did that. He recorded one of the hypnosis sessions so I could hear the tape as often as I needed to at home. It worked great. I felt happier, and I liked myself. After some time, he told me that I was now ready to go back in time. However, I was feeling so great about myself, I declined. I did not want it anymore.

I saw him many times. We worked together intensively, and then we would have a break. We had this agreement that whenever I needed more sessions, I could just call him, and he would make time for me. I learned a lot of valuable lessons from Christian, and I will forever be grateful for the time I worked with him.

Gradually, I felt better, and over the following years, I married Frank, and we had two children together.

CHAPTER 4

The Forgotten Trauma

Journal Entry, 2008
"Mom. Good morning, Mom." I hear Jonas, my six-year-old son, talking to me from a distance.

I try to wake up, but the left side of my body does not respond. My left arm and the side of my face feel numb, yet are burning. I cannot open my left eye.

"Dad, her eye is hanging again," Jonas yells. Frank walks into the room.

I open my right eye and see Frank and Jonas. They look concerned.

"Hi," I say, and pull all my energy together to try to wake up. I have been fighting a battle with my body for some time now. It seems like the left side of my body shuts down every time I sleep.

Now Cilia, my two-year-old daughter, runs in and I can feel a big wet kiss on my chin. "I love you." Her words just melt my heart.

The kids lay down with me, one on each side, and their giggles and jokes make me feel warm and grateful. My left eye starts to *open a little. My strength in the eye fights to overcome whatever it is that shuts me down.*

After some time, I can open it. It feels very sore, and it burns. But at least now I can open it, and the kids are not so scared to look at me anymore. My face still hangs a little on the left side, but in time, I will look normal again, and I will be able to go to work. My work has been very understanding, but I know it cannot continue like this. I am not functioning in the mornings, and I can't concentrate when I come to work. Sometimes, I will not be at work before lunchtime. And at home, I want to help out again—be a mom and a wife.

I have been hospitalized a few times now and the greatest doctors try to figure out what is wrong with me. Every time I talk to them, they suspect a new scary diagnosis and they run all different tests, but so far, they have not solved the mystery. My life is such a rollercoaster right now. The left side of my face and left arm hurts. The burning feeling inside makes me feel very uncomfortable and on edge.

"Ok, breakfast is ready. Let Mom have some rest so she can get better," Frank says.

I look at him. I can see how tired and worried he is, and I feel so bad about it. Nowadays, he is doing everything in the mornings for the kids until my body starts functioning, which can take anything from a few minutes to three-to-four hours. I cannot help feeling guilty and frustrated. Frank is such a great husband, he just does it all without complaining. But I know that this is hard on him too and on our relationship. I cannot be a wife to him right now or a mom for the kids. I feel like a burden to them. Even though he does not complain about it, I feel it. But there is nothing I can do about it. My body shuts down, and nobody knows why.

I hear how Jonas asks Frank all different questions about me. He worries, poor guy. I feel awful to put him through this. He is such a sweetheart. He should not sit and worry about his mom. I push myself to move my fingers on my left hand. I want to wake them up. It hurts, but I keep doing it. I want this to go away. My face feels strange. Some of my left side is still burning, some of it feels numb. I feel miserable. I am scared. How long will this continue? When is it going to stop? What is going on with me?

"Bye, Mom. Have a good day." Jonas hugs me. "You look better now."

"Thanks, my sweetie-pie." I feel better now. "Have a great day in school." I hug him. He is such a caring and good boy. He hugs me. I can feel how he does not want to let go. "I am going to be fine again, Jonas." I look him in the eye. "It will all be fine, I promise." He hugs me even more. "Now, go to school and have fun. I love you!" He hugs me for another few seconds and then he goes out to put on his shoes.

"Bye, Mom." Cilia is waving to me from the door, all dressed and ready to go to daycare. I look at her and smile.

"Bye, my love. Have a great day. I love you." I wave back at her and send her an air kiss.

Frank comes in and kisses me. He is in a hurry, taking the kids to school and daycare before going to work himself.

"Thanks for everything." I look at him with tears in my eyes. I feel so awful that he has to do it all, that I cannot help him.

"Don't worry," he replies. "Just get better, ok?"

My heart melts. I love him so much.

In 2006, about six months after Cilia was born, I experienced the first symptoms of my body closing down. They began on the left side of my face and in my left arm. Sometimes, I would feel numbness, at other times pain. In the beginning, it was very little, and I just thought it was because I was tired. I mean, I had just had a baby, and I was up during the nights. But it continued, and the mornings especially became very hard for me to manage. I was so tired and often I would not feel awake on the left side of my body, even though I was.

I went to the doctor, and he sent me to see different specialists at the hospital. The symptoms became more extreme. Now, the left side of my face could be swollen when I woke up in the mornings, and often I had a hard time opening my left eye. It could take from minutes to hours for me to get some kind of normal functioning on the left side, which is why Frank often had to deal with the kids in the mornings by himself. It was very stressful for him, and also for me. I was scared. It felt like my left side was shutting down, and I did not know why. I remember I could be lying in bed when my kids would jump into bed and kiss me good morning. I could hear them and see them, but I sometimes had a hard time responding. It was very frustrating. I so wanted to reach out to them and kiss them back and talk to them, but I couldn't. I felt paralyzed. I was alive inside the shell of my body.

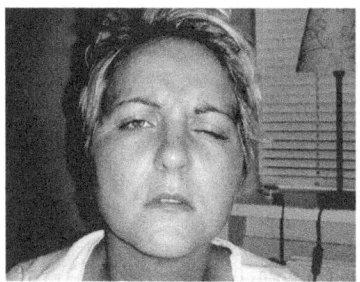 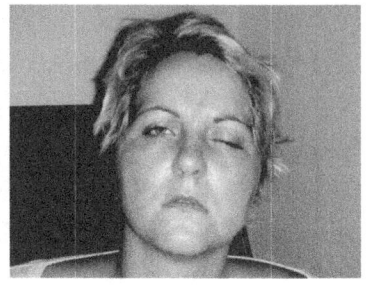

I was constantly tired, and I had a really hard time concentrating. In 2007, I started a new job, and I really liked it, but I just could not seem to do it right. It was a dream job. I had my own clients who I was in charge of. They were working in different businesses and I had meetings with them about the cars they were leasing for their employees from the company I was working for. I loved it. I just did a really crappy job. Everything was one big mess in my head. I could not remember anything, and I was in constant pain.

As always, I would pretend things were good. I would keep up my happy smile and work hard to do my best. But internally I was so freaking scared. What was happening to me? The doctors in the hospital carried out all kinds of tests as they tried to figure out what was going on with me. I was in and out of the hospital several times, which was very time-consuming and frustrating. Nobody could tell me what was going on, and all the tests came back normal. Nobody asked me about other things in my life. They just looked at the physical symptoms and the test results. The doctors did not reach any conclusion.

The symptoms disappeared for a while, but they came back in 2008. This time, the symptoms were worse, and now it was affecting my job. My commute was about an hour each way, and there was no way I could function well enough to drive for that long in the mornings. My workplace agreed that I could come into the office when I felt well enough to drive. But unfortunately, that meant that I could not keep my clients. They needed somebody to be there full time. Instead, I would help out in the office as much as I could. I was crushed, but I was grateful that I could still come in and do something. It helped me to be surrounded by my sweet colleagues, even though I felt like such a disappointment. And I felt like I was letting everybody down.

In 2009, the doctors finally diagnosed me with a rare kind of Focal Dystonia, and they prescribed medication to reduce the symptoms on the left side in the mornings. They told me that my kind of Dystonia did that every time I fell asleep, spasms would start in my brain, and the medication would help counteract them.

The day they diagnosed me was, unfortunately, the day after my employers had laid me off from my job.

CHAPTER 5

The Breakdown

In 2010, Frank got a new job, and we moved to California. This was a new start for our family, and we all liked it a lot. I felt so good; I was able to stop taking the medication.

In 2011, I had my first flashback of sexual abuse. It came out of the blue, and I felt I'd been knocked down. This was the first of many, and I did not really understand what was happening. Suddenly, I did not feel safe anymore.

My world turned upside down, and I had to face a past that I had blocked out. I did not know what to believe. The emotional and physical pain that I experienced was unbearable. My Dystonia returned. The left side of my body began closing down. Most mornings, I looked like a pirate again. I needed to get back on the medication.

I contacted my doctor, who referred me to a therapist. She told me they had a Trauma Recovery Group at the hospital for people with PTSD, and she wanted me to join it.

I met in a group every week. After the group session, I would go through the flashbacks in a safe environment together with one of the trauma therapists who was leading the group. The trauma recovery group was an eight-week program, but at the end of the eight weeks, I was not ready to leave, so they allowed me to take another month. Working on myself in the group was the first time I learned to ground myself and really listen to what was going on within me. They gave me tools to use when I had flashbacks and, for the first time, I was not running away from those hard feelings. The trauma recovery group helped me realize that I needed to speak up. The pain inside me was growing, and it was preventing me from functioning as a person.

Phone call with a family member, 2013
"Hi, there is something really important I need to tell you." I am nervous. My hands are moist, and I need to concentrate hard on not dropping the phone. I can hear my heart. It is beating so hard it's like somebody is stabbing me. I look out of the window. The trees are standing so firmly in the ground, unlike me. I am sitting in a chair; my feet are jumping around. It feels like I need to pee. I have already been to the bathroom five times. I try to sit still, but my body reacts like it is full of small animals jumping around. I feel sick. I feel cold. And I feel like throwing up.

"What is it? Are you ok? You sound awful," they say.

I know that they do not like any kind of problem. They want everything to be smooth. They run away from any kind of conflict; they always have. But I need to tell them this, and I really hope that they will listen to me.

"No, actually, I am not fine," I continue. My breathing is getting more and more difficult. "I need to tell you something very important. It is about something that happened to me when I was a child."

There is silence. It fills the room like a big balloon, just getting bigger and bigger, nearly exploding. I feel so dizzy and sick right now.

"I was sexually abused as a kid," I say. "I started remembering it. I had flashbacks. I have been in therapy for post-traumatic stress for the last couple of months as I try to figure out what this is all about."

The silence is unbearable.

"Are you there?" I feel a huge relief that I've told them but, at the same time, I am anxious about how they will react.

"Are you sure?" Their voice is low.

"Yes."

"Perhaps your memories are wrong?"

I am confused. "What do you mean?" I become annoyed with them. "What do you mean?"

"It is a very serious accusation you are making here."

"I know! That is why it is really hard for me to tell you." My heart beats very fast now. It feels like it might explode. "That is why I was sick. It was my body trying to tell me that I needed to remember this and deal with it."

"This is a lot for me to take in right now," they say.

"I understand," I reply. "I just wanted you to know."

"Let's talk another day, ok?" They hang up.

I sit in the chair and stare out of the window. The phone is still in my hand. I don't know what to feel. I am scared. I feel guilty. I feel relieved. I am so sad and so empty. This is such a nightmare.

I feel an arm around me. A nice comforting arm. Frank's arm.

"I am here for you. You are doing the right thing," he says.

I lean into him, and we sit like that for a while, staring quietly out of the window.

My extended family was shocked to hear how badly I was doing. Some of them told me that it was probably nothing and that I just needed to forget it or get over it. Others thought I was making it up, and they did not want to be in contact with me anymore.

When I went back to the group that week, I was crushed and told them about some of my extended family's reaction. It had taken such courage for me to share it with them, and I felt so low and confused. Now, I started doubting myself and feeling guilty. One of the therapists leading the group told me that, unfortunately, this was a very common reaction from families in such situations, but that she was proud of me for telling them. We talked about it in the group, which helped me.

Driving home from the group that evening was hard.

Journal Entry, 2013

I feel I have betrayed a part of my extended family. But I also feel so hurt that they don't believe me. It is dark and raining. I am crying. The anger and pain are bottling up in my body. I cannot take it anymore. I have a hard time focusing on driving. I cannot see the road from all the tears and rain. Why bother? What is wrong with me? I close my eyes. I just want peace. I don't want to feel this pain anymore. My head and my stomach are hurting. I am so angry with everything and everybody. "Go away, pain! Go away!"

I scream. I open my eyes. The rainy weather is crazy now. The windshield wipers are making a terrible noise. They move fast, as if they are trying to catch the rain. But the rain is faster.

The rain is heavy and loud, like the pain inside me. How can I escape this? There are trees on the side of the street. I could just speed up and hit one of them, and—BAM! Then it would all be over, and I could get some peace. I feel trapped. I feel hands all over me. They are crawling around my body like small ants. I want to get away from them.

"Go away!" I yell, while hitting myself. I want to die. I think of Frank and the kids. They are at home waiting for me. I pull to the side and cry. After a few minutes, I dry my eyes. I turn on some music, and I continue my way home. I have to get home to my husband and my kids. They are my family. I need to be there for them. They need me, and I need them.

It was extremely challenging to keep up a normal family life during this time. In therapy, I learned how to deal with the flashbacks, but when they showed up at home, I would break down on the floor and be so scared. Frank would sit with me, and in a calm voice, remind me that I was safe. This was his way of trying to bring me back to the present.

My therapist was wonderful. After the group, I would sit in her office. She would go through the flashbacks with me and help me try to understand all of this mess.

I tried to be a good mom. I was still volunteering in the school, and I tried to keep our daily life as normal as possible. Periodically, I took medication for my Dystonia, which made it manageable. But I was extremely tired.

I looked at my kids, and I just wanted them to be safe. I was going through a lot during those months. I was working hard on healing myself, dealing with all different kinds of emotions, as well as the sadness of losing contact with some of my extended family. All this, while trying to be a mom in a new country. The little child in me (my inner child) was screaming so hard, but I had to be a mom first. I could only take care of the little child within me when my own kids were sleeping.

Finally, on my last day of group therapy, I remember looking around. All these beautiful people had been like a family to me when part of my own extended family wasn't. I was closer to these people, who I had known only for a few months, than I had ever been to my extended family. Now what?

It was also the last day in the group for another woman, and she was clearly nervous, too.

"What am I supposed to do now?" she said. "Just go home and wait for my next depression?"

We laughed, but we both felt the seriousness of this. I had, over the last few months, understood why I had tried to numb my feelings for nearly all my life. I now understood the WHY. But I did not want to feel like a victim anymore. What should I do?

I had spent so much time in my life sitting in a therapist's office, complaining, blaming, not really knowing where to go. I had cried and felt sorry for myself.

It doesn't matter why I was stuck. It doesn't matter what my trauma was or who did what. Everybody's journey is different. We all go through stuff. What matters is what we do with it. I had had enough of it. I was so sick of feeling stuck and sorry for myself. I knew I needed to make a change.

CHAPTER 6

The Crossroad/The Change

In 2013, I started a new chapter in my life. After the PTSD treatment, I knew I wanted to use my newly gained knowledge of dealing with and healing from my trauma and turn it into something positive. This was bigger than just me. I had heard about life coaching, and I started researching different programs. When I talked to an admissions coach from the iPEC (Institute for Professional Excellence in Coaching) I had no doubts that this was the next step for me. So, I began a life-changing journey.

The program was a great combination of in-person and online learning, and it went deep. I had experienced a lot of therapy in my life, but this was exactly what I now needed to move on from all my therapy and build myself up again as a person. I had seen myself as broken for so long, and I needed something to turn my misery into victory.

The one-year program was the most developing and growing experience I have ever had. My trainer was an amazing person. He showed me and the other students what coaching could be. He challenged us in all different ways, to stretch us and help us grow.

I met the most amazing and warm people in the program. Some people were looking for their purpose and wanted to make a difference. I felt at home. Many of the connections from that time have turned into beautiful friendships.

In the program, we talked a lot about how you cannot change others, and I realized I was still blaming myself and other people. This was what was keeping me stuck. With practical steps, I learned to choose how I wanted to respond and act in situations or towards people, instead of reacting emotionally by default—something I had been doing all my life. I did not have to see myself as not good enough anymore. I had a choice. I could change what I believed about myself. I loved this! It was so freeing and empowering, and slowly I saw and felt the changes.

I changed a lot during my iPEC studying time and the time after that. I grew into a person who I respected and liked. Because of that, I became much closer to the people I was around. And I consciously chose to not be around other people. Instead of blaming myself or anybody else, instead of judging people or situations, instead of hating myself or feeling sorry for myself, I took a good look at my own role in every situation and relationship I was in. I took responsibility for my own life and choices. I started from scratch and decided who I wanted to be as a mom, a wife, a friend, etc. And I began to change myself.

The transformation was not easy and quick. I would rather describe it as a change of lifestyle with a learning curve. It was a new way of thinking, and I will continue to grow into it for as long as I live.

Instead of looking for acceptance and love from everybody else, I gave myself what I had been seeking and longing for all my life. I gave myself unconditional love. I told myself, "I love you, just because you are YOU!" A simple statement, yet so difficult to tell yourself and believe.

I don't have to do anything to be good enough. I AM good enough and I love myself, just because I am ME.

I realized how much of my life I had spent seeking approval from other people. It did not matter how much they told me that I was lovely or that they loved me. I didn't believe them.

When I finished all my assignments and coaching calls and was ready for the iPEC exam, I had one last session with my mentor. Right before our call, I chatted to a business coach regarding starting up my own coaching business, but that conversation did not go well. I was confused and unsure about myself after having spoken with him. He wanted me to pick only one niche to start the business, and I was struggling to figure out how to do that. Exactly what niche was I supposed to pick?

My mentor sensed I wasn't feeling right and asked what was going on. After telling her about my conversation with the business coach, and that I just did not know how to apply what he had tried to teach me, she said, "But Ingrid, you have never fitted in a box. Why do you try so hard now?"

There it was, right in my face! For this last year, I had been working on finding out who I was and who I wanted to be. I had gone through an incredible transformation. I could not be like everybody else, because I did just not fit in the box. Not even as a coach. I simply had to give myself permission to be ME. And that's what I did, and what I still do. Every time I feel stuck, I think of her words. I take a step back and reconnect to myself.

Journal Entry, 2014
Ingrid, you have never fitted in a box. Why do you try so hard now?

I spent years trying to find love and acceptance or just trying to fit in. But enough is enough! I am exactly as I am supposed to be. Nobody needs to tell me that I am good enough anymore. I am free to be who I am. I am the mom and the person that I want to be. No boxes to fit in. I am ME.

CHAPTER 7

Marriage and Family Life

I noticed changes as soon as I began my iPEC training. One time, when I came home from a coaching weekend, I sat down with Frank and said, "I just want you to know, I don't need you—instead I choose to be with you." Wow, what a powerful and new way to look at our relationship.

Frank saw me transform into a woman who was very different from the person I was when he met me. I had so often been sick and fragile, and many times Frank had taken on the role of caregiver. But now I found all these different sides of me, sides that he had never seen before. I didn't need him to take care of me anymore. I wanted him to see me as his partner instead. It was very clear that our relationship had to shift in one way or another, and we had many conversations around that. I did not want to go back to being the person I had been. Also, I wanted to see him as my husband and not my caregiver.

When I started changing myself, it also forced Frank to change, too. Our previous patterns did not work anymore. I responded or reacted differently to the way I used to. I liked the new me, and I know he also liked the new me. The old me was so used to depending on him, but the new me also challenged him a bit more.

Being dependent on Frank was a pattern I had seen a lot in my life. It was familiar to me. This is why it worked so well for me that Frank had been okay taking on the role of caregiver. However, that also meant I remained the victim, where I did not know who I could be. Now, I wanted to explore that. He was the man who took on that challenge. He always made space for me to do my thing, and he transformed in his own way. We grew individually and together as a couple. Our marriage transformed into a beautiful, deep respect and love for each other. Love now has a very different meaning. Love is what we want it to be. We choose each other.

It wasn't just my relationship with Frank that changed during that time. It was also my relationship with my kids. I spent a lot of time thinking about who I wanted to be as a mom. To do that, I had to connect with my own inner child (Little Me) to figure out what I had not gotten as a child, and what I had needed. There was a lot of healing that had to be done. How could I give my kids something I had never received myself?

The answer was this: being a parent made me go back and parent myself. As my children grew older each year, different things would trigger me. A different grief would come up. I needed to look at that because I wanted to give my kids a different kind of mom than the one I was. To do that, I needed to grow up myself.

This was an intense and challenging time because I could not just put my mom role on pause while I worked on my own healing. I had to be a mom, an adult, when my kids were around me, and then deal with all my old stuff and difficult emotions (Little Me) whenever I got a chance.

Through my coaching, I had learned new tools that helped me change the way I interacted with my kids. By letting go of control and judgment, I could meet them where they were at. I could let them be themselves, and I allowed them to feel whatever they were feeling, including difficult feelings like anger and frustration.

On those occasions where I would normally be scared of big emotions and typically numb myself, I now had to learn to sit with these feelings myself and to feel them. It was time to take responsibility and be the mom I wanted to be. Little Me learned in parallel with my own kids, and by allowing the difficult emotions to come out in a healthy way, by naming them, or writing about them, I could slowly heal my own scars while, at the same time, teaching my kids how to manage their difficult feelings.

Melting ice cubes in my hand was a great way to feel the pain from old anger instead of yelling, numbing, or self-sabotaging. During the day, I would act as a mom, hugging my kids and comforting them, and at night when they were asleep, I would hug myself, pretending I was hugging Little Me. It wasn't always easy. I called the hard days my growing days, and I had many growing days. Growing days were important though, because they were there to help me process, learn, and grow. They helped me break patterns and transform into being the mom I wanted to be.

One thing that was important to me was that my kids learned to respect themselves and listen to their bodies. Both my kids did martial arts at some point. One afternoon, when Cilia was in elementary school, I told her to put on her uniform, because we were supposed to leave for class. I finished up some things in the kitchen, packed my stuff, and then went into her room to see if she was ready to go. She was sitting on her bed. She had not changed into her uniform.

Normally, I would get annoyed and ask her to hurry up because I did not want her to be late or miss it. I could feel my stomach tensing. However, instead of getting annoyed with her, I chose another approach.

I sat down with her and said, "You are not wearing your uniform. Are you ok? How are you doing?"

Cilia replied, "Mom, it is so busy in school, we are making everything ready for the open house, and I am just really tired. My body is really tired."

I could feel the stress and anger build up as I thought about how much those classes were and how we would now be late. I took a deep breath, smiled, and said, "That sounds very stressful, so it makes sense that you are tired. I am proud of you for listening to your body and respecting it. Also, thank you for reminding me to check in with myself. I am also tired. How about we skip today, and you will go next time?"

Cilia looked up at me.

"What do you want to do instead?" I asked her. I could tell she was relieved. "Do you want to watch TV and eat some ice cream?"

We sat down on the sofa in the living room, each with a bowl of our favorite ice cream, mint chocolate chip, and watched some TV. After a little while, I felt her arm around my back, giving me a big hug. This was such a lovely moment. I would have missed this moment had I pushed her to go to class that day. Instead, I gave her permission to listen to her body. As parents, we need to model this. Too many times, we feel stressed and too busy to take a break ourselves. If you are tired, it is totally fine to lie down on the sofa to relax.

I wasn't always like that as a mom. Actually, I learned this from Cilia. She was that kind of child that would go to her room by herself because she wanted to be alone. She could spend hours playing with her small ponies or drawing. She was a natural in taking me-time.

At some point when Cilia was in elementary school, she became angry or had tantrums in the mornings before school. She was often grumpy and became annoyed about anything, and she was so slow. That made the mornings difficult for all of us. I did not want to be a yelling mom, so one afternoon I had a conversation with her about the mornings.

"Why do you think you get so mad in the mornings? What can we do to help you? What do you need?"

She thought about it for a while, and then she said, "Mom, in school, I always have people around me. That makes me very tired. Can we try that I have breakfast in my room in the mornings, so I can get some quiet time before school?"

I didn't know what to feel. In my head, it was important to have breakfast together as a family. That's what we do as a family. But how she explained it made sense.

"If that's what you need, then I think we should try it."

The next morning, she had breakfast in her room. We missed her at the breakfast table, but that morning she came out of her room with a big smile, ready to go to school, ready to face the world. She had breakfast in her room for a while, and eventually, she began joining us at the breakfast table again. She was learning to navigate being an introvert in a very extroverted world.

By respecting her own boundaries, she was being true to herself. That's pretty amazing at such a young age. Helping her embrace her introversion allowed me to learn about my own introversion. This was an aspect of myself that I had never learned or known about. I never learned to set boundaries or ask for what I needed. I never knew what I needed. That is why it was so important to me that we, in our little family, all felt seen and heard. We often had family meetings, and it's a model that gave us somewhere safe to share what we needed, ask for help, and set boundaries. We all need to feel seen and heard.

My son, Jonas, has always been a very caring guy. Soon after we had moved to the US, I will never forget his excitement when he came home from school and told me that over here the kids are rewarded for being good to others. His kindhearted way of being was perfect for this.

Unfortunately, the playground was not an easy place to navigate for a sensitive and good-hearted boy.

Jonas also taught me the beauty of not fitting in the box. He has always embraced being different. As a mom, I learned to see him for what and who he is, instead of comparing him to other kids or what society expects. As a parent, that can sometimes be challenging, but it has been a journey that I would not have missed. The courage he has shown in staying true to who he is and what he believes in has been super inspiring.

I have learned so much from both my kids. They were and still are my greatest teachers. Having let them find out who they want to be, having supported them in finding their own way, and not just following what society or anybody else expects of them, I also found myself. As my kids grew older each year, I saw and heard Little Me grow up in parallel with them. It is an absolute honor to be their mom, and I love them both so much.

Both my kids have grown into being very independent young people, going out into the world with curiosity and empathy. I know that, whatever challenges they face, they know how to listen inwards and look for solutions instead of focusing on problems. They live with the reality that life is hard sometimes. They have messed up and gotten themselves back on track, and they both have a stubbornness that keeps them going. But they also know it's okay to ask for help. In our house, there are no mistakes, only learning opportunities. Most importantly, they know they are loved unconditionally!

Looking back on my journey and seeing my life today, I feel gratitude. Has it been tough? Hell, yes! But I would not change any of it. This was my journey and, because of that, I am now the person I want to be. Every day I make a choice. It would be so easy to slip back into a depression or feel stuck or sorry for myself. But that is not who I want to be. I have shown my kids how to deal with hard situations. Has it been perfect? No. Nothing is perfect. And it is an illusion to strive for that. Life is messy and can be challenging. But if we see every day as a gift and if we live in the present instead of in the past or the future, life is pretty awesome.

Words cannot describe the feelings around my journey. But I hope you can hear my love for life. I have spent too many years, for whatever reason, numbing myself. Today, I choose to live to the full in every single day and every single moment. My journey has become my life-purpose, and I appreciate every single feeling that has helped me get here.

CHAPTER 8

My Thoughts

What have I learned from my journey? And why am I sharing it with you?

Many adults come to me because they feel that something is not working in their life. They blame the boss, the spouse, the kids, themselves, etc. and they want me to fix it. They live in a reactive mode and are extremely stressed and alert. Slowly, we get to the cause of it when we start working together. They see the parallels with their childhood, learn to deal with the triggers and, with time, they learn to love themselves as they are. Because of that, their environment changes too. It can be a lonely process. Sometimes they realize they have attracted people in their lives who keep them in the old pain and pattern. Or they realize they self-sabotage or are attracted to other people's drama.

Many adults with childhood trauma are triggered when their kids reach the same age they were when the trauma happened, but they don't understand that this is where it comes from. The same is the case in many relationships. It's so much easier to blame the other person and want them to change, instead of looking at ourselves and understanding our reactions.

Finding peace with ourselves works best when we are surrounded by positivity. Some people will change with you. Some won't. Change is not for everyone. Sadly, many people thrive in the pain because they are stuck in familiar feelings.

Being stuck in the past and, because of that, being diagnosed with eating disorders, anxiety, depression, PTSD, or other psychological challenges, is a really lonely journey. Loneliness is often what these people know too well in the first place. That is why it's so easy to get stuck in the system. Support groups are great. They make you feel that you belong, and you are understood. Maybe for the first time ever. So why move on from that? It's like a little family, and you want to stay.

The same feelings can arise when you see a therapist. Many people see their therapist for years. There is nothing wrong with seeing a therapist. I often refer my clients to a therapist. But they tend to stay there even when they have worked through their issues, either because the therapist is more like a friend who you meet up with weekly, or they are stuck with a therapist that is simply not the right fit for them. As you know, I tried that, and had I not been strong enough to go against what she was asking of me, I would not be married to Frank today. One of my therapists clearly had a problem with men in general, so she wanted me to not like my boyfriend. Sometimes it feels like you have to be strong and lucky to meet the people that are right for you, which can be really hard when you feel miserable.

I think that the mental health system, in general, can do a better job in helping people move out of the system again, and not just into the next support group or the next diagnosis. If you stay in the system, it makes you feel special in one way. You become your diagnosis and you have your people around you who understand you. Your safety net. But it can also make you feel that you are too sick or too scared to move on with your life. That is a big problem.

When I started my business, I reached out to a lot of therapists to introduce myself, hoping they would like to collaborate with me. Some resisted. It felt like they were scared I would take their clients away. I was stunned by that. One of them actually told me that they would not refer to me unless I studied for a specific examination. I might not have a PhD or a long therapist education, but I have lived through what I am talking about, and I have helped myself make it out to the other side. That is one thing that my clients love about me. I still believe that the best way to help clients is when therapists and coaches work together. Therapists can help with the deep healing, while a coach can offer practical steps and accountability to help clients return to normal life—one with a mindset that they are a lovable person, not a broken one.

Another problem is that there are often long waiting lists for treatment. I was lucky to have a doctor who saw me as a person and took the time to talk to me every week until

I could start treatment. It would be a wonderful resource to have somebody who could do that for everyone who is waiting to start treatment.

I often wondered how to respond when my kids told me about how they learned to be good to others in school. I believe that, as an adult with childhood trauma, it is really important to look at what we are modeling to our kids. Some adults grew up in environments that made them become pleasers and/or overachievers. Of course, it's important to help others, but if you don't help yourself too, you will become overwhelmed and experience burnout. Perhaps today, some kids are drawn into numbing behaviors on their phones and drugs because they experience a lot of stress and expectations around them, sometimes from their parents. I think many kids today have parents who have experienced childhood trauma and because of that have become pleasers and/or overachievers. It is important for the parents to see their kids as they are, and help them find themselves. Our kids are not here to live out our dreams. I also think it should be mandatory for schools to teach kids more about self-awareness, boundaries, and how to take care of themselves and others in a healthy way. I believe helping them become a whole person would make a big difference in the younger generation.

It's also important to know that there are some kinds of trauma you may not remember until much later in life. That is what happened to me. I blocked out all memories of the sexual abuse, but my body remembered.

It would also benefit adults with childhood trauma if the physical medical sector worked more closely with the mental health sector. Doctors need a more holistic view. When my doctors tried to figure out why my body had the physical symptoms it had, nobody asked me what else was going on in my life. Not once did they ask about the eating disorder treatment or how I was doing. I felt really bad during those years. Sometimes I felt they didn't believe me because all the tests came back normal. I felt like a problem to them, which I struggled with, being someone who was always trying to please people. Not a good combination at all. In fact, that just made matters worse, knowing that I did not want to be a problem.

Because of my own experiences, I believe there is a connection between childhood trauma, mental health, and physical symptoms. In 2014/15, I started my coaching business, helping people who are stuck in trauma or past hurt to dream again. Here, I have seen this connection with many clients as well. I wanted to bring this awareness to future doctors, so since 2017, I have been sharing my story with medical students at California Northstate University. Over the years, I have also shared my experiences with treatment centers specializing in eating disorders and substance abuse to inspire patients there to work on themselves and believe in a brighter future.

I hope my story can influence people working in the mental health and medical fields so that they, with this awareness, can better help the many adults that are struggling today without knowing why. I wish that in the future, there is a greater collaboration between the different mental health and medical sectors to connect the dots and see the bigger picture in the patient's life.

The healing journey can be long, so if I can help just one person shorten theirs, then it is worth my own journey.

CHAPTER 9

Aftermath

If you are an adult who has experienced childhood trauma, it is important to know that you are not alone. There are many of us.

If you feel stuck in an old trauma, you should know that there is a way out. The loneliness and the pain you are feeling emotionally and physically can be treated. But it starts with you. I have spent so many years of my life blaming myself and others. But that is not a full life. Actually, that just gives other people more power. Every time you react, you give away your power. I want you to know that you can take that power back. But you have to *want* it. You can expect more of yourself, and you can push yourself further, because nobody will do it for you.

I am sharing my journey to show you that it is possible to heal from childhood trauma, move forward, and live a wonderful and happy life. Be aware, though, not to get stuck in your healing journey. Always focus on getting better. It's so easy to get caught up in the medical and mental health system. It's important to find therapists and doctors who work for you.

It is also important to realize and ask questions about how your mental and physical health are connected and can be trauma-related. I spent too many years being stuck, believing that somebody would come and rescue me. I used my sickness and diagnosis as an excuse to not live my life. I wasted years holding on to anger and blame. Old pain just grew bigger and made me physically sick. I am no longer willing to let old pain take over my life. I cannot get all those years back. But I can share my story here and hope that at least one person will learn from it.

If you keep focusing on the negatives, such as what you don't have and all the things that have happened to you, then you will not see what you do have and all the good in your life. Remember, every day we get is a gift.

My past has shaped me to be the person I am today. And a lot of the strength I have in me is because of my past. I am not angry with anybody anymore. I was, for many years. But I have forgiven them, and I have forgiven myself. If I had not been through all the things I have, I could not be the mom, wife, or person that I am today. By facing my demons and changing myself, my Dystonia disappeared. Today, I very rarely feel it, and when I do, I know it's my body telling me to listen inwards and take care of myself.

Healing from trauma is not a quick fix. I still have hard days. I still have days when I don't want to get out of bed, or when I feel lonely and sad. It would be so easy to slip back into old patterns. But every day we have a choice.

We only have one life. You can create the life you want to have. You can choose to live your life to the fullest, every day.

It's time to let go of the mask. It's time to fill yourself up with unconditional love. It's time to break patterns. It's time to stop being a patient and become a person. You have a choice. And it is up to you to decide how you will live your life.

If you feel stuck in old pain and hurt and feel
ready to change your life, please go to my website
and see how I can help you.
www.abildpedersencoaching.com

ACKNOWLEDGMENTS

cheering me up, and reminding me why I needed to write this book. I could not have done it without your support. I am so blessed to have you, special people, in my life.

There are many other very special people to thank. Friends and colleagues who have such a special place in my heart: Alifya, Anja, Brianna, Christina, Desiree, Dhara, Elliot, Emilie, Fabienne, Helene, Jill, Judy, Kathleen, Kirsten, Monica, Nicole, Patty, Stella, Steven, Tiffany, Tzeli, Valerie, Victoria, Whitney, and Yonit—and so many more. Thank you for being you. You are all so awesome, and I am so happy to have you in my life.

Last, but not least, there is my new family: Christine Kloser and her wonderful team at Capucia Publishing. When I first met with Carrie, I had no doubts that this was the right place to help me publish my book. You welcomed me into your publishing community in such a warm and loving way, it really felt like a family—a safe environment to birth this very personal book. Thank you so much!

Thank you to all of you! (Including those who I have not mentioned here.)

asked so many wonderful questions, and I am confident that you all will become great doctors and make a big difference. Talking to you and sharing my story has been a big push to write this book. Seeing your responses made it clear to me how important it was to share my journey.

A big thank you also goes to all my doctors and therapists who have helped me when I needed it. Nothing can explain the pain that comes with trauma. I am so grateful to all of you for having given me a safe place to cry and heal. I especially want to thank my therapist, A. You have been by my side since my first flashback. You were the one who inspired me to heal through writing. You were right. It was the right thing for me to do. Thank you for that and for always being there for me.

Then there's iPEC, my second family. You came into my life when I needed more practical tools to help me move from victimhood to victory. We can heal and work on ourselves all our life, but at some point, we need to move forward and redesign our life. This is what you helped me do. You challenged me to take an honest look at myself and make the necessary changes so I could take responsibility and make conscious choices. It changed my relationship with everything and everybody. I will forever be grateful for that.

Some days have been full of self-doubt and fear. Thank you to those special people in my life who I know I can call at two in the morning. My chosen family: Franzi, Ginnie, Jacqui, Judi, Lory, Renee, Shelyna, Signe, and Taylor. Thank you all for always being there for me, listening to me,

ACKNOWLEDGMENTS

First of all, I want to thank my husband. He has been my rock since I met him. If it wasn't for him, I would not be here today. And then there are my beautiful kids, Cilia and Jonas, my biggest teachers in life. Being your mom has been, and will always be, my biggest honor. This little family, my husband and my kids, is why I have been strong and able to push through the darkest times. Thank you for helping me see the light when I did not see it myself. Thank you for being my inspiration to take on the fight and change myself to become who I am today. I love you all unconditionally!

I also want to thank all my former and current clients. I am so amazed by your courage to grow and change. You are all such an inspiration. Thank you for allowing me to be part of your journey. You all rock!

Thank you to the different interim clerkship directors at California Northstate University for allowing me to share my story with your medical students since 2017. It means so much to me to share with future doctors the connection between trauma and physical symptoms that I have experienced. Every time I talk with your student group, I feel that my journey has a purpose. I also want to thank all the medical students that I have talked to. You have

ABOUT THE AUTHOR

Ingrid Christine Abild-Pedersen is the owner and founder of Abild-Pedersen Coaching and a speaker. She is a certified professional coach, and an Energy Leadership™ Index Master Practitioner, trained by the Institute for Professional Excellence in Coaching.

Ingrid, who has lived in Denmark, Germany, and England, now lives in California (USA). She is working with both national and international clients on breaking patterns and building leadership in their own lives. Additionally, since 2017, she has served as a guest lecturer for California Northstate University, teaching medical students about the connection between trauma and physical symptoms.

ingrid@abildpedersencoaching.com
www.abildpedersencoaching.com

Made in the USA
Las Vegas, NV
19 September 2023